The Little Book

D1522242

The Little Book

Conceptual Elements of Research

Marino C. Alvarez and D. Bob Gowin

ASSOCIATION OF TEACHER EDUCATORS AND

ROWMAN & LITTLEFIELD EDUCATION

A division of

ROWMAN & LITTLEFIELD PUBLISHERS, INC.
Lanham • New York • Toronto • Plymouth, UK

Published by Rowman & Littlefield Education
A division of Rowman & Littlefield Publishers, Inc.
A wholly owned subsidiary of The Rowman & Littlefield Publishing Group, Inc.
4501 Forbes Boulevard, Suite 200, Lanham, Maryland 20706
http://www.rowmaneducation.com

Estover Road, Plymouth PL6 7PY, United Kingdom

British Library Cataloguing in Publication Information Available

Library of Congress Cataloging-in-Publication Data

Alvarez, Marino C. (Marino Carlos), 1941–
   The little book : conceptual elements of research / Marino C. Alvarez and D. Bob Gowin.
      p. cm.
      ISBN 978-1-60709-293-3 (pbk. : alk. paper) — ISBN 978-1-60709-294-0 (electronic)
   1. Research—Methodology. 2. Academic writing. I. Gowin, D. B. II. Title.
   Q180.55.M4A428 2010
   001.4—dc22   2009028599

The paper used in this publication meets the minimum requirements of American National Standard for Information Sciences—Permanence of Paper for Printed Library Materials, ANSI/NISO Z39.48-1992.

Printed in the United States of America

Contents

Acknowledgments

We are indebted to our students for using this research strategy when conducting their research and writing research reports in high schools, and to our undergraduate and graduate students who have written their master's theses and doctoral dissertations using this guide. When preparing this book, we asked several to review and make suggestions to make this a readable, practical, and meaningful book. We are grateful to those students who did so. Special recognition is given to Stephen Baird, a public school teacher and doctoral student; Dr. Sandra Keown, a public middle school teacher and adjunct college professor; Audrey Lukula, instructor, Academic Enrichment, Advisement, and Orientation Center, Tennessee State University; and doctoral students Maria L. Edlin, assistant director, Center for Economic Education, Middle Tennessee State University, and Cassie Zippay, a literacy instructor at Western Kentucky University. We would also like to thank Maera Stratton and Melissa McNitt from Rowman & Littlefield Education.

We thank the editors of Cambridge University Press for permission to include portions of writings and appendix II of our book, *The Art of Educating with V Diagrams,* by D. Bob Gowin and Marino C. Alvarez.

Introduction

Desultory readers are seldom remarkable for the exactness of their learning.

—(A Study in Scarlet)

Our intent for this book is not to trivialize the research process, but rather to provide a companion guide to the research process. This book is a companion piece to research texts. We realize that engaging in the research process can be intimidating especially to those who are experiencing the journey for the first time. While there are many research texts that provide comprehensive descriptions of research methods, designs and qualitative and quantitative analyses, this book is intended to guide you through a personal path of inquiry that will enable you to better understand the concepts and facts that go into planning, carrying out, and finalizing a research investigation.

Our aim is to provide you with a framework to focus and conduct a research investigation from its inception to its resolution, and beyond. We advocate managing knowledge versus managing time. In so doing, you are better able to assemble relevant documents and materials that are necessary to address your research question rather than spending time on tasks that may or may not be appropriate or meaningful. We advise you to make use of your prior knowledge and experiences in this research process.

You are the center of the inquiry so think about questions that are interesting to you and stimulate your interest and curiosity. Your questions will take new directions depending on how you structure your events and select your records. Changing the question changes the events and the records, so similar investigations do not necessarily result in similar findings. You may ask a question that upon reaching a resolution does not as yet have an answer. This provides you with an opportunity to create new questions, make extended hypotheses based on your findings, and also make an unrealized possibility a reality.

Our book takes you on a path of inquiry by asking questions for you to answer. During this process the path you take will become better understood by using the question markers as road signs toward your resolution. Reflecting on your questions, events, theory, and records of events that are happening at the time they are taking place, will enable you to better conceptualize the findings.

Research is mostly a conceptual matter. Thinking with concepts is the main effort of the researcher. But, "facts," as records of events, are very important. Records are what the thinking is about because recordings are not subjective, they are objective, the "objects." Recordings can be repeated, over and over again. They support the thinker's claims about reality. These three golden keys—events, records of events (facts), and concepts—are three different realities. The thinking researcher combines realities by giving meaning to events. Meanings are both subjective and objective. The working researcher understands that research helps us to *grasp meanings not our own*. Meanings are the stuff of learning. We learn meanings. Both inquiry and learning come together during the processes of researching.

As you proceed with your research project, note taking becomes very important. Recording the events that you encounter will enable you to better make sense of what is happening along the way. As you record a thought or a fact keep the notes organized. Be cognizant of these three triads: "naming events" (use of concepts to name an event that is happening); collecting the facts/recordings; and showing how concepts, facts, and events are meaningfully connected.

Each chapter begins with a Sherlockian quote from the pen of Arthur Conan Doyle. Since Sherlock Holmes is the greatest detective, who uses the powers of observation and formulates value questions to guide his inquiry, we use these quotes to provide you with a "mindset" for reading and engaging in the research process. Just as a detective seeks to unravel a mystery through evidence and explanation, so too, does a researcher use similar elements by formulating a question, paying attention to an event, and making records of what is happening *at the time it is happening.*

We introduce a research strategy diagram and research phases that contain questions as a framework to take you through the process. This research strategy diagram and its components directly relate to the **V** diagram, which we advocate using during the research process. The appendices show a researcher checklist and a researcher/mentor checklist that contain each of the research phases, and can be used by or with high school students, undergraduate and graduate students, or teachers doing individual or collaborative action research projects. Also, concept mapping is described as a way to conceptualize and reveal your ideas so that they can be shared with others to enable the thinking process that your research investigation demands. These tools have been used by high school and postsecondary students in our projects. To better understand the **V** diagram, we direct you to read our book, *The Art of Educating with V Diagrams,* which provides a comprehensive description of the uses of the **V**.

Brevity in this text is intentional. Efforts to provide succinct questions and invite pauses for reflections are designed to focus and expedite the research process. As stated earlier, we ask that you evoke your prior knowledge and experience in this process and not rely solely on inputs from other resources. We believe that if you take the time to think, reflect, and answer the questions we pose, as well as actively engage in the use of concept mapping and **V** diagramming, that your research experience will be rewarding and provide pathways for future research endeavors.

List of Figures

Chapter 1

Preliminary Ideas, Diagrams, and Tools to Focus and Expedite Your Research

The interplay of ideas and the oblique uses of knowledge are often of extraordinary interest.

—(The Valley of Fear)

Answering and Reflecting on the Questions
Research Phases and Questions
Research Strategy
Tools for Thinking
Concept Mapping
V Diagrams
Q-5 Technique
Value Questions

ANSWERING AND REFLECTING ON THE QUESTIONS

We strongly suggest that you first read this book in its entirety from cover to cover in order to familiarize yourself with the conceptual framework and related questions of each chapter. Next, as you begin to conceptualize your research question and assemble your documents and materials, take time to reflect on each research phase and the research strategy diagram. The respective questions for each research phase are important for you to consider.

It is a mistake to skim over the questions and stray from the process in your eagerness to reach a final product. This will add to your "time" and diminish the value your research investigation affords.

Save time by managing knowledge using the tools in this book:

- Constructing and revising concept maps.
- Constructing **V** diagrams.
- Using the Q-5 Technique to evaluate documents.
- Answering the questions within each phase and reflecting on your thoughts and progress along the way.

RESEARCH PHASES AND QUESTIONS

The Research Strategy Phases and Questions provide an overall framework of the research process:

> Problem/Situation: Plan/Strategy → Course of Action → Resolution → Action

Within each phase are questions that guide you in the development of the problem, the design of the investigation, the treatment of the findings, and subsequent reflections for further inquiry. We suggest you read and react thoughtfully to these questions. Your writing time will be reduced and the goal of learning for a purpose will become a reality.

RESEARCH STRATEGY

The Research Strategy is a way to guide your research investigation.[1] It is a strategy rather than a rigid framework. The components interact to aid you in planning, carrying out, and reaching decisions in your investigation. A diagram of the Research Strategy appears in Figure 1.1. Chapters 2–10 provide a detailed question guide that relates to elements shown in the Research Strategy.

This Research Strategy constitutes a plan of action. Review this diagram starting from the top and taking time to think about each of the areas as you navigate your way down. To help prepare your progress with this Research Strategy here are some tools to start your idea building: a concept map, a **V** diagram, and the Q-5 Technique.

TOOLS FOR THINKING

Concept Mapping

A hierarchical concept map is a visual representation of an individual's thought processes. It is a word diagram that is portrayed visually in a hierarchical

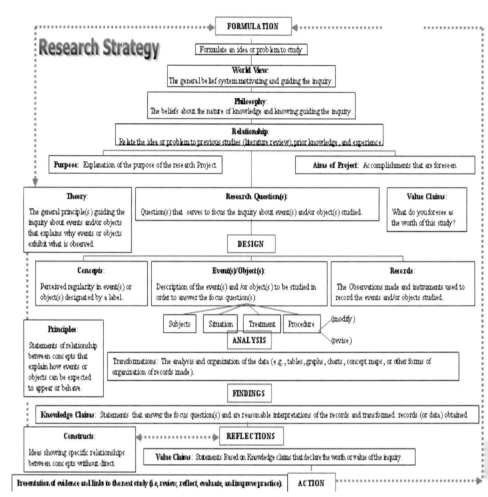

Figure 1.1.   Research Strategy

fashion and represents concepts and their relationships. These concept maps are developed and used as a way to visually display and share ideas.[2]

Why Concept Maps in the Research Process?

As you have just read, it is very important to organize and clarify your ideas when planning and carrying out your research plan. A stumbling block in the preliminary stages is not being able to take a topic and reduce it to a manageable question to study. Concept maps aid in this process by revealing our thoughts on our topic in ways that focus the question to its

Figure 1.2.   Two Concepts Linked by a Proposition

events. *A good practice to remember is when beginning a concept map, write a focus question and use this question to guide your ideas in its development.*

> When reviewing the literature, and thinking about a topic, much material is amassed that needs to be sorted into categories relevant to the question being asked. These maps, and the revisions that occur, enable us to rethink and refocus our ideas as we go through this process.

The *key* to a hierarchical concept map is the *propositional link* between two concepts. How well ideas are represented and understood is determined by the word or word phrase that links two concepts. For example, "Sky is Blue" is indicated by the word "is" at the time it is represented (See Figure 1.2.). Later it may be that the "Sky is Gray" or the "Sky is Cloudy" or the "Sky is Overcast."

Words that are used in the linking propositional phrase are keys to identifying misconceptions or faulty linkages among and between concepts. This is why the importance of using concept maps in the preparation, carrying out, and finalizing of your research agenda are necessary. For example, high school students in our Exploring Minds Project develop and revise concept maps as they engage with their research investigations. These maps guide students when making decisions, self-monitoring their progress and enabling them to assess what is happening during the course of their study.

The maps you construct and revise clarify your understanding of your topic and question. They also provide a visual representation to share with someone else who may be a mentor or a person knowledgeable in the topic you have chosen. As you, and perhaps another, view each map and study the relationships being represented and the relevance of the words *linking* these ideas, the clarity of these ideas are crystallized and better understood by you to make your investigation more meaningful in its pursuit and resolution. A concept map shows the interrelationship between ideas, facts, and details. A hierarchical concept map progresses from most inclusive (general) ideas to least inclusive (specific) ones.

Making A Map

The following steps are for developing a concept map when preparing a research investigation:

1. *Select* a topic and decide upon the most important idea to which all other concept words can be related. Put this key concept in the top-center of your paper. Think about how other concept words can be related to this central idea. (Brainstorm your thoughts.) Make a listing of each of these concepts on a sheet of paper.[3]
2. *Rank* these concept words hierarchically from most inclusive (general) to least inclusive (concrete and specific). Eliminate the ones that do not pertain to your key concept.
3. *Arrange* the concept words on your paper according to hierarchical structure and relationship. For example, arrange concepts that can be subsumed and/or related to each other. As you post each concept, simultaneously *link* each of the concept words by drawing lines showing the connections among and between the ideas. Label each line using a word or word phrase to explain the relationships. If an idea relates to others that have already been represented in another portion of the map, show the relationship of this idea by drawing a broken line to indicate cross linkage. Once you complete your first effort, take time to examine your arrangement. At this time, you may want to rearrange or redo your map. You also may add other concepts to the arrangement.

Let's follow a high school student's initial planning using concept maps to formulate his research study with "Black Holes."

The first map constructed by the high school student had too broad of a topic, "The Life of a High Mass Star," of which "Black Holes" was a part of many areas (see Figure 1.3). In this map, ideas are linked by labeled lines that contain either a word or word phrases to show their relationship. This is referred to as a *proposition*. Propositions are meaningful relationships between concepts and are expressed by a connecting line and linking word(s). A proposition is a statement in which a relationship between two concepts is affirmed or denied, so that it can therefore be significantly characterized as either true or false.[4] Propositions are important indicators that can point to misconceptions or faulty linkages between concepts that may need to be revised.

He then reexamined the research topic and focused his inquiry to "Black Holes." He then constructed another map as shown in Figure 1.4.

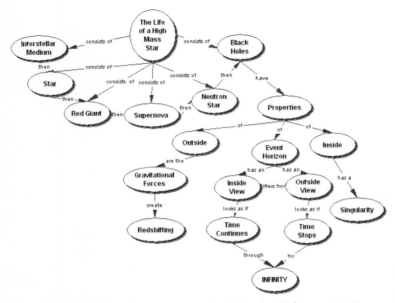

Figure 1.3.   First Concept Map: "The Life of a High Mass Star"

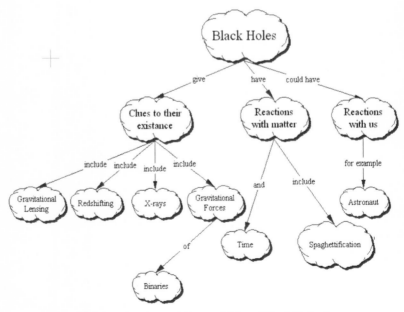

Figure 1.4.   Second Concept Map: "Black Holes"

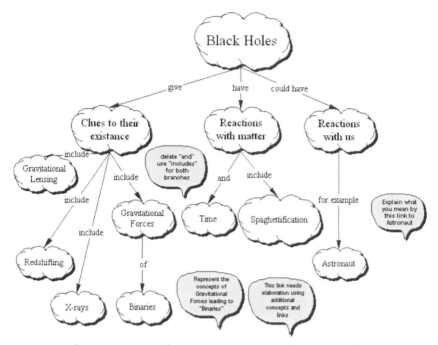

Figure 1.5. Second Concept Map Reviewed: "Black Holes"

After completing this second map, he shared it with his teacher. His teacher provided feedback by writing on his map (see Figure 1.5). The teacher provided feedback on the map itself and a third map was revised and reconstructed.

4. *Review* your concept map. Look again at your concept map. Can you add any other information to the map? Can you think of another way that this map can be developed?

   The student reviewed the feedback and then constructed a third map shown in Figure 1.6.

5. *A Concept Map as a Template for Writing.* Once a concept map is constructed, writing about the visual display is an easy task due to the labeling and linking of the ideas in the arrangement. Better comprehension gives greater meaning to a concept.[4] *Write* a paragraph(s) describing the conceptual arrangement of the map. This is a relatively easy process since the map is now organized into coherent and unified threads evolving from a focus or theme.

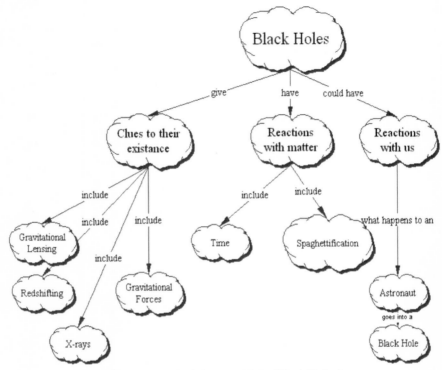

Figure 1.6.   Final Concept Map: "Black Holes"

Let's Review These Concept Mapping Steps:

1. Make a personal concept map by mapping an event that is *happening now!*

    • In your life.
    • In the paper you are planning to write.
    • In an extracurricular activity.
    • In your work experience.
    • In your preliminary research topic.

2. Once you select an item, be sure to: *Write your Focus Question.*
3. Now, start following the steps given above and make your map.

Concept maps, connecting questions and events, are extremely helpful. Do not be afraid to construct a dozen or more concept maps at this point. Clarifying conceptual thinking is as difficult as it is significant for the progress of research. Reconceptualizing ideas by remaking your map enables better understanding of your topic and focuses your research question. By sharing your concept map with another enables you to better ascertain if someone else understands your thinking with the topic. A dialogue clarifies any misconceptions or faulty linkages that are represented; thereby providing you with a clearer path of inquiry.

V Diagrams

Another tool to aid your research planning is the **V** diagram. The **V** heuristic was developed by Bob Gowin (1981) to enable students to understand the structure of knowledge (e.g., relational networks, hierarchies, and combinations) and to understand the process of knowledge construction. Gowin's fundamental assumption is that knowledge is not absolute, but rather it is dependent upon the concepts, theories, and methodologies by which we view the world.

Why Use the V?

Our principle for using the **V** diagram in the research process is: *The V diagram mediates conceptual and methodological research design and practice.* Planning a study requires the selection of a research method or procedure that best reveals the answers to the questions posed. Research is a systematic process of collecting and analyzing information for some stated purpose, and various research methods are used when conducting research. The **V** is a tool that can help us understand and learn. Since knowledge is not discovered, but is constructed by people, it has a structure that can be analyzed. The **V** helps to identify the components of knowledge, clarify their relationships, and present them in a visually compact and clear way.

To learn meaningfully, individuals relate new knowledge to relevant concepts and propositions they already know. The **V** diagram aids this linking process by acting as a metacognitive tool that requires users to make explicit connections between previously learned and newly acquired information. The **V** diagram is shaped like a "**V**" and elements are arrayed around it. The left side, conceptual or thinking side, of the **V** displays *world view, philosophy, theory,* and *concepts.* The right side, methodological or doing side, has *value claims, knowledge claims, transformations,* and *records. Events and/or objects* are at the point of the **V**. Both sides are interactive; not exclusive as shown in Figure 1.7.[5]

Emily Mofield is a public middle school teacher who earned her doctoral degree using these tools. During her planning process she developed a

Knowledge V Diagram

CONCEPTUAL/THEORETICAL		METHODOLOGICAL
(Thinking)		(Doing)

WORLD VIEW:

The general belief and knowledge system motivating and guiding the inquiry.

FOCUS/RESEARCH: QUESTIONS

Questions that serve to focus the inquiry about events and/or objects studied.

VALUE CLAIMS:

Statements based on knowledge claims that declare the worth or value of the inquiry.

PHILOSOPHY:

The beliefs about the nature of knowledge and knowing guiding the inquiry.

THEORY:

The general principles guiding the inquiry that explain why events or objects exhibit what is observed.

PRINCIPLES:

Statements of relationships between concepts that explain how events or objects can be expected to appear or behave.

CONSTRUCTS:

Ideas showing specific relationships between concepts, without direct origin in events or objects.

CONCEPTS:

Perceived regularity in events or objects (or records of events or objects) designated by a label.

KNOWLEDGE CLAIMS:

Statements that answer the RQs or FQs question(s) and are reasonable interpretations of the records and transformed records (or data) obtained.

TRANSFORMATIONS:

Tables, graphs, concept maps, statistics, or other forms of organization of records made.

RECORDS:

The observations made and recorded from the events/objects studied.

EVENTS AND/OR OBJECTS:

Description of the event(s) and/or object(s) to be studied in order to answer the research or focus question

Figure 1.7.   Gowin's V Diagram Components

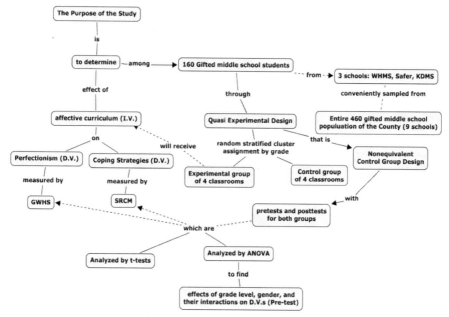

Figure 1.8.   Emily's Concept Map

concept map and a **V** diagram. The map shown in Figure 1.8 represents her initial thinking about some of the components in the "Plan/Strategy" that served as preliminary discussion points.

   She begins to formulate ideas that surround her thinking about the problem she is going to investigate. Preliminary ideas relate to her research question that focuses on an "Affective Curriculum" for gifted students.

   Emily also used the **V** diagram as another tool to plan and finalize her dissertation study. In Figure 1.9 her initial **V** diagram is shown. Notice that she has begun the formative stages of the Research Strategy: Plan/Strategy and Course of Action.

   She has her research questions that relate directly to the events of the study. The concepts, events, and records (facts) are in place. The left side (thinking side) of the **V** diagram reflects the ideas that are guiding her investigation, and the right side (doing side) of the **V** diagram shows what she believes the worth of the study will accomplish (value claims) and how she plans to represent her data. Notice that the Knowledge Claims (the answers to the questions) are not stated since the study is yet to be undertaken. This **V** provides the user with a sound organizational plan, and once the study is completed, a template from which to write and discuss the overall investigation.

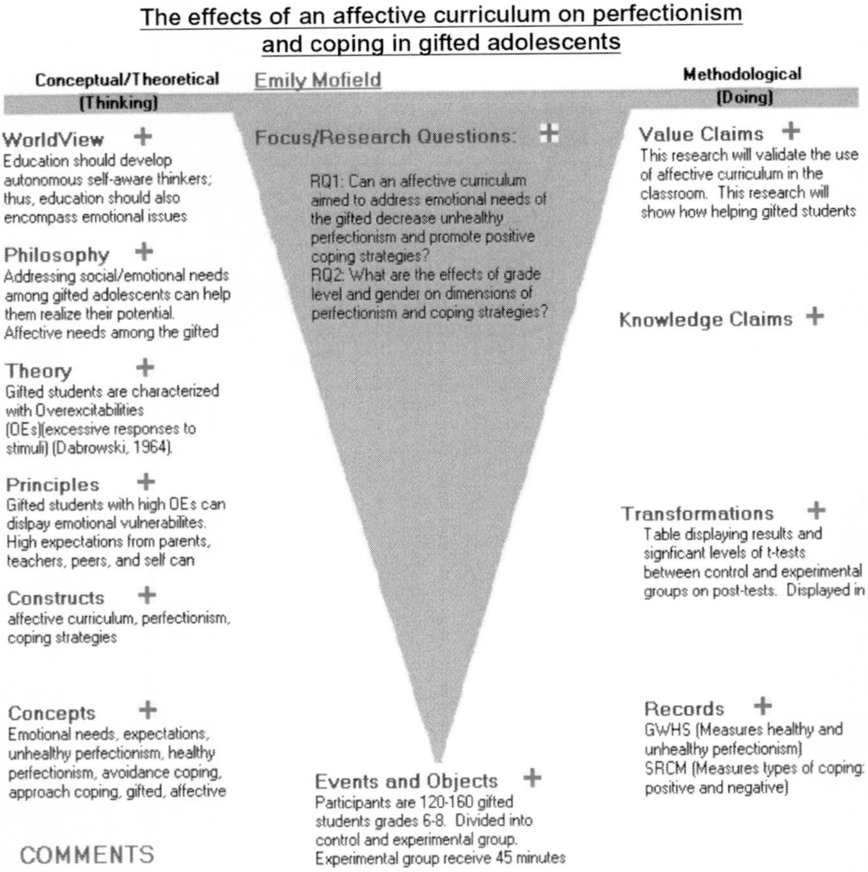

The effects of an affective curriculum on perfectionism and coping in gifted adolescents

Conceptual/Theoretical   Emily Mofield   **Methodological**
(Thinking)   **(Doing)**

WorldView ✛
Education should develop
autonomous self-aware thinkers;
thus, education should also
encompass emotional issues

Focus/Research Questions: ✛

RQ1: Can an affective curriculum
aimed to address emotional needs of
the gifted decrease unhealthy
perfectionism and promote positive
coping strategies?
RQ2: What are the effects of grade
level and gender on dimensions of
perfectionism and coping strategies?

Value Claims ✛
This research will validate the use
of affective curriculum in the
classroom. This research will
show how helping gifted students

Philosophy ✛
Addressing social/emotional needs
among gifted adolescents can help
them realize their potential.
Affective needs among the gifted

Knowledge Claims ✛

Theory ✛
Gifted students are characterized
with Overexcitabilities
(OEs)(excessive responses to
stimuli) (Dabrowski, 1964).

Principles ✛
Gifted students with high OEs can
dislpay emotional vulnerabilites.
High expectations from parents,
teachers, peers, and self can

Transformations ✛
Table displaying results and
signficant levels of t-tests
between control and experimental
groups on post-tests. Displayed in

Constructs ✛
affective curriculum, perfectionism,
coping strategies

Concepts ✛
Emotional needs, expectations,
unhealthy perfectionism, healthy
perfectionism, avoidance coping,
approach coping, gifted, affective

Records ✛
GWHS (Measures healthy and
unhealthy perfectionism)
SRCM (Measures types of coping:
positive and negative)

COMMENTS

Events and Objects ✛
Participants are 120-160 gifted
students grades 6-8. Divided into
control and experimental group.
Experimental group receive 45 minutes

Figure 1.9.   Emily's V Diagram

Q-5 Technique

This is a tool to help you analyze documents during your literature review.
The Q-5 technique is a series of questions that helps to evaluate the degree of
conceptual and factual makeup that forms a particular document

> Q-5 functions as a code-breaker when analyzing documents and
> research reports. It is a quick way to break into the often daunting
> boiler-plate-like knowledge claims of published research. A Q-5 brief
> scan can save time and effort in one's review of the literature. Q-5 is an
> excellent way to begin one's effort to understand any work.

Cracking the code is an enabling step forward in one's own learning. Using Q-5, shown in Figure 1.10, can give you the sense of the coherence and the quality of the document being analyzed.

Five key questions asked and answered about any given set of knowledge claims can give us a shorthand technique to grasp the knowledge's structure and worth of a document.

1. *What is the question(s)?*
   FQ—Focus Question
   RQ—Research Question

Write the question(s) the author is using to guide the document. There may be times, however, authors do not write out their guiding questions.

Q-5 Technique As Code Breaker

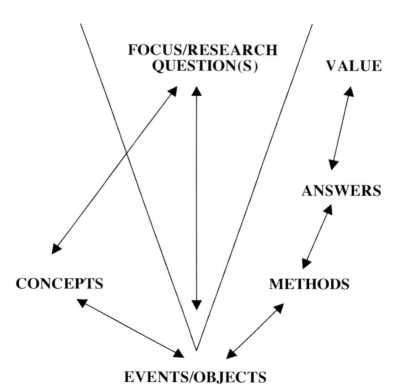

Figure 1.10. The Q-5 Technique as Codebreaker

You need to be alert to what is often missing. Read directly looking for the explicit or implied questions the author must have asked in order to supply the answers (knowledge claims) found in the published articles and books. Question-asking is central to inquiry. As you read the document ask yourself: What is the telling question of the work? What does it tell on, or about?

2. What are the key concepts?

This question expands into the whole left side of the **V** with its concern with conceptual structure. Questions are formed by connecting concepts. All questions contain concepts. Any piece of research is framed by a structure of concepts. These sets of concepts indicate the thinking required for the inquiry to continue. The conceptual structure shapes and guides (gives meaning to) the ways one seeks answers. A strong theory impels inquiry questions and methods. What are the key concepts? What concepts are needed to ask the question?

3. What methods are used?
   If Ss were used, who were they and how did they participate in the events?
   What events or objects were the focus of the question(s).
   Records: What instruments were used to collect the "facts" of what was happening in the events being studied?

This question expands into the whole right side of the **V**, especially the lower left with its close tie to events and objects and ways of making records of these events. Methods are modes of inquiry. They are the ways used to construct answers (knowledge claims). Methods are "HOW" questions: How do we find out something? How do we proceed? How do we make facts? How do we transform facts into data? Methods are so important to inquiry that they often overwhelm others parts of inquiry. What methods were used to answer the telling question? What methods are useful in answering the question or questions? How am I going to find out what's happening?

4. What answers are presented?
   Do the findings directly answer the questions that were asked at the beginning of the study?

This question expands into the top levels, knowledge claims, and the key functions of claims—interpretations, generalizations, and explanations. Inquiry closes when facts, data, and knowledge claims are completed.

These claims are often named "Conclusions." It is as if nothing more needs to be done. The important role of knowledge claims is to supply a fertile source of new inquiry questions. What are the major knowledge claims of the work? What answers are produced? What new questions can be asked?

5. So what?

This question expands into value claims. What is the value? What value claims can be made given the knowledge claims presented? It enables the user of the **V** to take a look at the coherence of the **V**, at the ways parts feed into other parts. What value claims are made in the work? *Instrumental, Intrinsic, Comparative, Decision, and Ideal*

VALUE QUESTIONS

An important aspect of any investigation is the worth that is derived from the initial intent and the final evaluation. Value claims are statements based on the knowledge claims that declare the worth or value of the inquiry. Value claims are answers to value questions. We believe only five value questions are enough to span the field of value claims.

1. *Instrumental Value Question.* Is X good for Y?
2. *Intrinsic Value Question.* Is X good in itself?
3. *Comparative Value Question.* Is X better than Y?
4. *Decision Value Question.* Is X right? Ought we choose X?
5. *Ideal Value Question.* Is X as good as it can be, or can it be made much better ideally?

When planning this book, all of these value claims were taken into consideration.

1. Instrumental Value Question. Is X good for Y?
   Will writing this book enable persons to better understand the research process?
   Is the information contained within this book good for focusing and expediting the research process?
   Is the information within this book good for conceptualizing ideas?
2. Intrinsic Value Question. Is X good in itself?
   Is this book the best way to inform persons interested in conducting research?

Will this book aid the reader to learn *with* the information they will encounter?

3. Comparative Value Question. Is X better than Y?

   Will using this book as a companion to a research text enrich the learning and understanding of the research process?

   Will research findings generated from the use of this book better enable users to conceptualize and represent findings of their research?

4. Decision Value Question. Is X right? Ought we choose X?

   Is it right that research methodologies and practices be imposed by professors, teachers, or outsiders with little consideration by the student? Should topics, theory, research procedures and/or practices be prescribed in a master's or doctoral program? A high school or undergraduate senior project?

5. Ideal Value Question. Is X as good as it can be, or can it be made much better ideally? Is this book as good as it can be?

NOTES

1. This research strategy and the phases were first used with high school students in the Exploring Minds Project, Tennessee State University, and appeared in Marino C. Alvarez, *Researcher's Notebook: A Resource for Faculty, Staff, and Students* (Nashville, TN: Center of Excellence in Information Systems), 2000.

2. For a comprehensive description and examples of varied uses of concept maps see Joseph D. Novak and D. Bob Gowin, *Learning How to Learn* (New York: Cambridge University Press), 1984; Joseph D. Novak, *Learning, Creating, and Using Knowledge: Concept Maps as Facilitative Tools in Schools and Corporations,* (Mahwah, NJ: Lawrence Erlbaum Associates), 1998; Marino C. Alvarez in Walter Pauk, *How to Study in College,* 4th ed. (Boston: Houghton Mifflin Company), pp. 212–219, 1989.

3. Electronic software programs are available to construct concept maps. The "Black Holes" maps were constructed using Inspiration software. A free program for students and educators that we recommend is Cmap Tools (http://cmap.ihmc.us/conceptmap.html).

4. This definition for "proposition" was retrieved from *Dictionary.com Unabridged (v 1.1)*. Retrieved March 25, 2009, from Dictionary.com website: http://dictionary.reference.com/browse/proposition.

5. For a fuller understanding of the **V** diagram, its epistemic elements, and its uses as a teaching, learning, and researching tool, see D. Bob Gowin, *Educating* (Ithaca, NY: Cornell University Press, 1981); also D. Bob Gowin and Marino C. Alvarez, *The Art of Educating with V Diagrams* (New York and Cambridge, UK: Cambridge University Press, 2005).

I

PROBLEM/SITUATION

Drawing by Frank Wiles of Sherlock Holmes reading a book in "The Adventure of the Veiled Lodger," appearing in *The Strand* Magazine, February 1927.

Chapter 2

Getting Started

The game is afoot.

—(The Adventure of the Abbey Grange)

You have a problem that needs to be resolved or a situation that needs to be addressed. Relate the circumstances of the research problem to your own prior knowledge and/or experience, and to other courses you have taken or are presently enrolled. Approach this research problem as an opportunity to learn and to make a new piece of knowledge from an existing body of known information.

STARTING POINTS

1. *Formulate an idea or a problem.*
2. *Brainstorm ideas.*

1. Formulate an idea or a problem to address your research topic. Write it on a sheet of paper, a 3×5 card, or a document using your word processing system.
2. Brainstorm ideas. Try *timed writing.*[1] Give yourself six minutes to write. Open the mind to the possibilities and put them on paper. Once you start the timer write anything that comes to mind. You must write complete sentences on this topic and your pencil or pen cannot stop moving. If you become stuck, write your first and last name over and over until another idea comes to mind; then continue with your writing. At the end of the

time period, take a look at what you have written. A few key ideas will emerge for you to think about.

NOTES

1. Marino C. Alvarez, "Sustained timed writing as an aid to fluency and creativity," *Teaching Exceptional Children,* 15, (3), 160–162, 1983. Timed writing has been used successfully to enable ideas to spontaneously emerge, and upon reflection, be crafted into a meaningful topic. We have also used timed writings to assess students in our Exploring Minds Project with their knowledge of a research topic under study.

Chapter 3

The Quality of the Question

We must look for consistency.

—(The Problem of Thor Bridge)

Several ideas from your timed writing and brainstorming activities have prompted some questions for you to consider that focus on your research thread. Now comes the most important part of your research study: the Question.

1. *What's your question?*
2. *Why is this question important to you?*
3. *How will answering this question fulfill your curiosity?*
4. *What do you need to do to answer it?*

1. WHAT'S YOUR QUESTION?

This question is of paramount importance in this first phase of your investigation. The quality of this question "sets the stage" for your research inquiry and determines the educational worth of what you want to accomplish. When using the **V** Diagram the middle is the place to write your question.

Ask yourself:

- How important is it to know more about this problem/situation?
- Have I read about this situation/problem before?

- Based upon what I have read or experienced how can I apply what I already know or have experienced to this problem/situation?

   And finally,

- How can I make this problem/situation *interesting* for me?

2. WHY IS THIS QUESTION IMPORTANT TO YOU?

What is it about this question that you feel is necessary to know and understand? Why is it an important question to ask?

3. HOW WILL ANSWERING THIS QUESTION FULFILL YOUR CURIOSITY?

The notion that stimulates a research study is the quest toward finding some kind of resolution or furthering the knowledge that we now hold with future events. What is it about this question that stirs your imagination and, if resolved, will add to your knowledge and perhaps that of the field?

4. WHAT DO YOU NEED TO DO TO ANSWER IT?

What factors need to be taken into account in the *Events* portion of your study to answer your question(s)? Such considerations include the resources you will need to assemble, persons to consult, the persons and/or apparatus you will need in your study, the environment in which it will take place, and the *records* you will need to monitor what is happening *at the time it is happening.*

II

PLAN/STRATEGY

The shaded Plan/Strategy phase shown on the following page begins your thinking about the "what," "why," and "how" for preparing your investigation.

What? *Formulation, Relationship, Purpose, Aim of Project, and Research Questions (Hypotheses).*

Why? *World View, Philosophy, Theory, Principles, and preliminary thoughts about the Value Claims that form the basis for your investigation.*

How? *Concepts, Events, and Records needed to answer a pertinent question(s).*

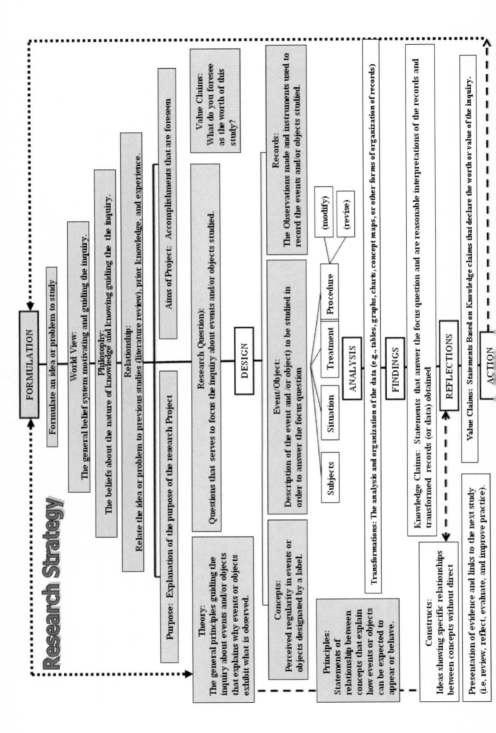

Chapter 4

Formalize Your Idea or Problem

It is not really difficult to construct a series of inferences, each dependent upon its predecessor and each simple in itself.

—(The Adventure of the Dancing Men)

1. *Formalize your idea or a problem.*
2. *Structure your research questions that need to be asked.*
3. *Events of your study.*
4. *Begin developing a Concept Map of your study.*
5. *You may wish to begin using the **V** Diagram to plan your investigation.*

1. Formalize your idea or a problem by narrowing your topic to a manageable area of inquiry that can be investigated. Begin by asking yourself questions that need to be answered. Ask yourself:

   • Is this an interesting idea or problem to investigate? If so, what are the key reasons for engaging me in this study? (List them underneath the idea or problem on your paper.)

2. What research questions need to be asked? Start formulating your research questions by directly relating them to your events/objects. Now is the time to check if your research question(s) is congruent with your events. If not, your research plan is going to go awry. Clarifying these two components, the *question and the event,* are the critical initial steps in any study. *Rigor occurs when the design of the research meets the question.*[1]

3. Events of the study. Include the relevant persons, apparatus, environment, situations, materials, resources, procedures, and so forth that will comprise the ways to answer your research question(s).
4. Begin developing a *concept map* of your study. Include pertinent ideas that you have written. This is the time to either use paper-and-pencil to draw your map, 3×5 cards to arrange your map in a hierarchical order, or an electronic tool such as Cmap Tools (refer to Chapter 1).
6. You may wish to begin using the *V Diagram* to plan your investigation. Now is the time to begin using the Research Strategy and its related phases to start your **V** diagram. You will find this tool to be an enabler as you proceed with your research process.

NOTES

1. Schuler W. Huck and William H. Cormier, *Reading Statistics and Research,* 2nd ed. (New York: HarperCollins), 1996, Preface.

Chapter 5

Relationship

There is nothing more deceptive than an obvious fact.

—(The Boscombe Valley Mystery)

Relate the idea or problem to previous studies (literature review), prior knowledge, and your experience.

ASSEMBLAGE

1. Literature Review
2. Aims of the Study
3. Questions to Consider

One of our primary aims is that you make use of prior knowledge and experience in this research process. After all, it's your study and you should be fully invested in developing, implementing, reaching some resolution, and presenting your thoughts based on your findings for future research implications.

1. Literature Review

Don't let reading the literature review fill you up! Take time to relate what you already have experienced and know about the problem or situation as you read and think about what others have written and reported. Remember to use the Q-5 Technique (refer to Chapter 1).

As we have suggested so far, it is important to explore new ways of thinking without abandoning one's own experience in the process. This powerful
notion expressed by Alfred North Whitehead (1939) makes the point that
before learning can begin we need to assemble materials in a very special
manner.[1] Assemblage denies systematic ways to arrive at predetermined out-
comes at the expense of understanding and refutes repetition of the known.
The notion of assemblage is that each of us starts with ideas predicated on
our own prior knowledge and world experience rather than starting with a
formulaic, systematic procedure when asking questions, solving problems,
and delving into research investigations. This happens when gathering origi-
nal sources, reading and viewing other related source materials, comparing
and contrasting points of view, analyzing cause and effects, activating our
own experiences, and providing opportunities for us to "show" what we can
do. Two tools we suggest for revealing your ideas in this research process
are concept maps and **V** diagrams (refer to Chapter 1).

The type of research project you choose will determine the extent of
your literature review. The following process may seem endless as you read
through the steps; however, this knowledge management process will prove
to be a time-saving process. Which articles to read and use and which sources
to quote that relate to your inquiry seem to be daunting tasks. However, practice with the following techniques will enable you to discern the usefulness
of the sources you encounter.

1. *Read about your idea or problem in journals that report related studies.*
2. Use the *Q-5 Technique* to evaluate an article or document. Then, use the
   V Diagram to analyze a seminal report by "laying the **V**" on the document.[2]
3. Make notations of a given study:

   a. *Convert the answers in the findings into questions.* Are these questions
      related to the ones that were hypothesized or asked in the research ques-
      tions at the beginning of the study?
   b. The sources they discuss in the introduction.
   c. The purpose or the problem being studied.
   d. The kind of method used in the study.
   e. The ways in which the information was gathered to answer their
      research questions.
   f. How the information was analyzed when reporting their results or
      findings.
   g. What the author(s) said about these findings.

4. What information in this report relates to your questions or concerns?
5. Was it written in a readable fashion?
6. Can you relate your prior knowledge and experience to this report?
7. Are their any questions that you feel are not answered in this report? If so, what would you have done to make the report more understandable?

2. Aims of the Study

Reflection Points

Let's take time to rethink the "why" and "what" you are doing. "Why" are you interested in this topic? "What" is the major focus of your research investigation? Based upon your understanding of what you already know coupled with what you have read or viewed, give an explanation of what you are trying to discover. Clarify your thinking (write it out.)

3. Questions to Consider

- Is your purpose for conducting this study to the point?
- *At this point* what do you foresee the direction your investigation taking?
- What *course of action* are you thinking about?
- Does this *course of action* give you direction for accomplishing your *Purpose?*
- *Value claims:* statements that declare the *worth* or value of this inquiry. What *potential* value do you see resulting from your study so far? "What's it good for?"
- *Research questions:* question(s) that serves to focus the inquiry about event(s) and/or object(s) studied. *This is important!* Is your research question stated in a clear fashion? If a few peers or colleagues were to read your research question, would they agree on the meaning of the key words? Reread this question. Would they?

  - Do you need to write a second research question (RQ2) that relates to your *purpose and aim?*
  - Limit the number of research questions you ask. It is better to answer one, two, or three well-thought research questions than to make an extensive listing.

- How do you plan to go about designing your study?

NOTES

1. Alfred North Whitehead. *Modes of Thought* (New York: Macmillan Company), 1939. Assemblage is an important process in the research planning and gathering of relevant sources and documents for evaluation.

2. See the Q-5 Technique and **V** Diagram components in D. Bob Gowin and Marino C. Alvarez, *The Art of Educating with V Diagrams* (New York and Cambridge UK: Cambridge University Press), 2005. "Laying the **V**" is a term used to describe using the **V** diagram when evaluating a document to reveal the coherence of a document, and informs the reader as to its educational worth.

Chapter 6

Where Do I Stand?

I have no data yet. It is a capital mistake to theorize before one has data. Insensibly one begins to twist facts to suit theories, instead of theories to suit facts.

—(A Scandal in Bohemia)

No question is asked, or event designed, studied, or interpreted, in isolation. All research is influenced by the researchers' own views, the "conceptual goggles" through which the work is viewed. The researcher's philosophies, theories, and perspectives lead to asking certain questions, to designing a particular event that they think will provide answers, and to interpreting the data in a particular way.

Take a Moment: State your thoughts and feelings concerning your world view and philosophy for the study.

When using the **V** diagram keep in mind that the left-side of the **V** contains important, and often neglected, components of research. The **V** challenges researchers to be more explicit about and aware of the role that their world view plays in their research by forcing them to really think about the philosophies, theories, principles, and concepts that are guiding their research. The components on the left side, therefore, interact with those of the right side of the **V** diagram.

1. *My World View*
2. *My Philosophy*
3. *Theory*
4. *Principles*
5. *Revise your concept map.*

World View: *A world view is the general belief system motivating and guiding the inquiry. Think about your idea or problem. Ask yourself:*

1. What are my views about this idea or problem? List them.
2. How do others perceive this idea or problem? (Students, parents, administrators, teachers, researchers, community members, members of the local board of education, members of the state department, federal government, state and national organizations, other countries.) List them.

Philosophy: *The beliefs about the nature of knowledge and knowing guiding the inquiry.* Ask yourself:

1. What are my beliefs about this idea or problem as it relates to the direction that this inquiry will take? List them.
2. What do others think and feel about this idea or problem? List those that you know about as well as those philosophical entries that you perceive others hold.

Theory: The general principle(s) guiding the inquiry about events and/or objects that explains *why* events or objects exhibit what is observed.

1. What idea(s) is guiding your study?
2. What assumptions are you testing?
3. Are these assumptions related to the events and/or objects that you are studying?

Principles: Conceptual guides to action in events. An action is a behavior with meaning. Principles are written statements of regularities in events. Principles combine knowledge claims and value claims. They are related to the theory being tested in the research investigation.

III

COURSE OF ACTION

During the shaded course of action phase shown on the following page, the selection of a research design begins to emerge. Key questions to consider are:

- *Do the events directly provide evidence to the research questions being asked?*
- *Are the concepts listed representative of the research questions and the events?*
- *Are the records chosen appropriate for monitoring the events?*

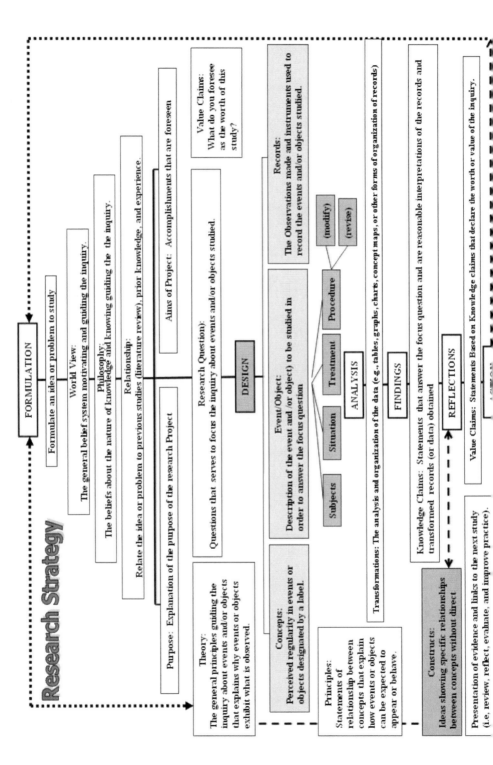

Research Strategy

FORMULATION

Formulate an idea or problem to study

World View: The general belief system motivating and guiding the inquiry.

Philosophy: The beliefs about the nature of knowledge and knowing guiding the the inquiry.

Relationship: Relate the idea or problem to previous studies (literature review), prior knowledge, and experience.

Aims of Project: Accomplishments that are foreseen

Value Claims: What do you foresee as the worth of this study?

Purpose: Explanation of the purpose of the research Project

Research Question): Questions that serves to focus the inquiry about events and/or objects studied.

DESIGN

Records: The Observations made and instruments used to record the events and/or objects studied

(modify)
(revise)
Procedure
Treatment
Situation
Subjects

ANALYSIS

Event/Object: Description of the event and /or object) to be studied in order to answer the focus question

Transformations: The analysis and organization of the data (e.g., tables, graphs, charts, concept maps, or other forms of organization of records)

FINDINGS

Knowledge Claims: Statements that answer the focus question and are reasonable interpretations of the records and transformed records (or data) obtained

REFLECTIONS

Value Claims: Statements Based on Knowledge claims that declare the worth or value of the inquiry.

Theory: The general principles guiding the inquiry about events and/or objects that explains why events or objects exhibit what is observed.

Concepts: Perceived regularity in events or objects designated by a label.

Principles: Statements of relationship between concepts that explain how events or objects can be expected to appear or behave.

Constructs: Ideas showing specific relationships between concepts without direct

Presentation of evidence and links to the next study (i.e. review, reflect, evaluate, and improve practice).

Chapter 7

Course of Action

The world is full of obvious things which nobody by any chance ever observes.

—(The Hound of the Baskervilles)

Be systematic in answering your own questions, gathering materials, and interviewing persons. Where do you need to visit? Who are the persons you need to interview or consult (e.g., other teachers, librarians, community persons, family relatives)? Where can you locate the information you need (e.g., school library, public library, college/university libraries, databases, community agencies, newspapers, state departments, government agencies, museums, archives, information on the World Wide Web)?

RESEARCH DESIGN

1. *Revisit your research questions.*
2. *Events/Objects*
3. *Concepts*
4. *Records*

1. Revisit your Research Questions

It's a good idea to revisit your research questions to be sure you are on track. Remember we wrote in Chapter 3 how important the quality of the research question is for your research investigation.

Events, Objects, and Facts

During this phase of your *research strategy* it is important that the event(s) and/or object(s), concepts, and records correspond directly to the research question(s) you are asking.

Event(s)/Object(s): Describe the event(s) and/or object(s) to be studied in order to answer the research question(s).

1. Keep in mind the meaning of these terms: event and object.

    -   Event—Anything that happens, can be made to happen, or is within the realm of possibility to happen.
    -   Object—Anything that exists and can be observed.
    -   Fact—a record of an event. Facts are *made* in the process of recording events.

How are you going to arrange the purpose or focus of your study in a way(s) that answers your research question(s)? Would a consensus of judges (teachers, scientists, professors, experts) agree that this is an educational event?

2. *This is important!* Write a brief description of the design or plan of the events or objects.
3. Does your description of the event(s) and/or object(s) clearly state what you will be investigating?
4. Is your description clearly stated so that it correlates with the research question(s) you asked?
5. Do you need to restate the research question(s) so that they directly relate to these event(s) and/or object(s)? If so, rewrite them now. (At this point you may find this to be redundant. You may have rewritten or altered the research questions several times. However, it cannot be overemphasized the importance of asking a critical question so that it is congruent and can be answered by your stated events.) Compare your research question(s) to your description of the event(s) and/object(s). Do you feel satisfied that this description will answer your question(s)?

Concepts

Concepts are perceived regularities in event(s) or object(s) designated by a label. A concept is a sign or symbol that points to regularity in events or objects.

1. Concepts are usually identified by words, but they may be numerical or symbolic, such as musical notations, chemical notations, iconic symbols, and mathematical symbols.

2. List the terms that need to be operationally defined in your paper.
3. Do these terms directly relate to the Research Question(s) you have asked, and to the description you have written under Event(s) and/or Object(s)?
4. The key concepts and telling questions become the tools for thinking both about the events and the claims made about the events.

Records

The observations made and instruments used to record the events and/or objects studied are the records.

1. Are the instruments you have listed going to accurately make a record of what you are asking and what you are doing in this study?
2. Do you need to add or discard any of your instruments?

Constructs

Constructs are specific relationships between concepts that serve to organize your ideas. *Make a concept map showing these concepts and their relationships.*

RESEARCH DESIGN

You are now ready to finalize your research design. *Review* your event(s) and/or object(s). Does the research question(s) directly relate to these events/objects? Do the concepts, and records correspond directly to the research question(s) you are asking and what you are going to do under events?

1. Do you need to restate the research question(s) so that they directly relate to these event(s) and/or object(s)? If so, rewrite them now. (This should be the last time, unless you have a proposal meeting when this question may arise again.)
2. Compare your research question(s) to your description of the event(s) and/object(s). Do you feel satisfied that this description will answer your question(s).
3. *Records:* Review your records.

   • Are the records valid and reliable?
   • Do you need to add or discard any of your instruments?
   • Do the concepts, principles and theories relate to your record making devices that assure validity and reliability?

4. *Concepts*: Look at these terms again. Do these terms relate to the research question(s) you have asked, and to the description you have written under Event(s) and/or Object(s)?
5. *Constructs:* Make a concept map of the left side of the **V** Diagram.

DESIGN DESCRIPTION

Write a description of your design or plan.

IV

RESOLUTION

The Resolution phase shown on the following page is the culmination of your research investigation.

First: List the findings from your Records of the Events.

Next: Select an appropriate way to visually display these findings by Transforming them into a chart, graph, table, figure, and so forth.

Then: Make interpretations of these transformations by listing them as Knowledge Claims. These knowledge claims are answers to your research questions (hypotheses). Each Research Question (Hypothesis) should have a corresponding Knowledge Claim.

Finally: Reflect on your knowledge claims and state your Value Claims.

Research Strategy

FORMULATION

- Formulate an idea or problem to study

World View: The general belief system motivating and guiding the inquiry.

Philosophy: The beliefs about the nature of knowledge and knowing guiding the the inquiry.

Relationship: Relate the idea or problem to previous studies (literature review), prior knowledge, and experience.

Purpose: Explanation of the purpose of the research Project

Aims of Project: Accomplishments that are foreseen

Value Claims: What do you foresee as the worth of this study?

Theory: The general principles guiding the inquiry about events and /or objects that explains why events or objects exhibit what is observed.

Concepts: Perceived regularity in events or objects designated by a label.

Principles: Statements of relationship between concepts that explain how events or objects can be expected to appear or behave.

Constructs: Ideas showing specific relationships between concepts without direct

Research Question: Questions that serves to focus the inquiry about events and/or objects studied.

DESIGN

Event/Object: Description of the event and /or object) to be studied in order to answer the focus question

- Subjects
- Situation
- Treatment
- Procedure
  - (modify)
  - (revise)

Records: The Observations made and instruments used to record the events and/or objects studied.

ANALYSIS

Transformations: The analysis and organization of the data (e.g., tables, graphs, charts, concept maps, or other forms of organization of records)

FINDINGS

Knowledge Claims: Statements that answer the focus question and are reasonable interpretations of the records and transformed records (or data) obtained

REFLECTIONS

Value Claims: Statements Based on Knowledge claims that declare the worth or value of the inquiry.

ACTION

- Presentation of evidence and links to the next study (i.e, review, reflect, evaluate, and improve practice).

Chapter 8

Resolution and Reflection

There is nothing like first-hand evidence.

—(A Study in Scarlet)

1. Analyze the event(s) and/or object(s) conceptually.
2. Transformations
3. Findings—Knowledge Claims
4. Reflections—Value Claims

ANALYSIS

Analysis: Analyze the event(s) and/or object(s) conceptually. Use your Records of the Event/Object to analyze your findings.

1. Make sense of the event. Ask yourself: "What's happening?"
2. What ideas (concepts) are taking place?
3. Does the idea arise from new knowledge?
4. What key idea is surfacing that can be connected to the event, or part of the event you would call a fact?

TRANSFORMATIONS

The analysis and organization of the data (e.g., rankings, tables, graphs, charts, concept maps, or other forms of organization of records made). Take these facts and put them in some order.

1. Make a summary judgment of these facts by writing them in a paragraph. Be sure to include in this summary how the concepts, principles and theories guide your record transformations. The choice of any graph or table, or the choice of certain statistics, should be influenced by your guiding principles.
2. Make a judgment on the criteria used and the way you *selected, ordered,* and determined *significance* from the collected data.
3. Be sure to make reliability checks at each point: selection, order, and significance.
4. If you use some kind of statistical or descriptive analyses you need to transform the data into a table, graph, chart, etc.).
5. When interpreting your records think of the best way this information can be displayed to show what you have found?
6. Does your visual accurately display your findings?

FINDINGS

Knowledge Claims

Statements that answer the research or focus question(s) and are reasonable interpretations of the records and transformed records (or data) obtained.

1. For each research question (RQ) there must be an answer.
2. Carefully evaluate your knowledge claims in relation to the research question(s) asked and your events(s) and/or object(s), records, and transformations.
3. Ask yourself: "What rules need to be followed when answering the research question(s) in light of what I have learned from the event(s) and/or object(s), records, transformations, and knowledge claims?"
4. Does your answer correspond directly to the question(s) asked?
5. Do you understand your answers to the Research Question(s) asked?

Check Principles

1. Review your k*nowledge claims.* Have your previously stated *principles* changed?
2. Do the principles show *how* your event(s) and/or object(s) appear to behave?
3. Do you need to rewrite the principles?
4. Do the principles still relate to the *theory* you stated?

Check Theory

1. Have your *knowledge claims* altered, supported, or negated your *theory?*
2. How will you report this theory that guided your inquiry in your research report or paper?

REFLECTIONS

Value Claims: Statements based on knowledge claims that declare the worth or value of the inquiry.

> Value claims are the educational worth of your study. These value claims are significant so think about them in a serious manner. Value judgments are always a significant part of the process of making knowledge claims. Value claims are answers to value questions, and are important considerations for any research outcome. Value (educational worth) determines the effectiveness of any study.

How does this study impact your future research? To answer this question you need to reflect on the findings and begin to weave a longer thread in this research. You need to find ways of making sense of the data you have gathered and interpreted in order to extend your understanding and meaning with this event. We believe only five value questions are enough to span the field of value claims (see Chapter 1):

1. Instrumental Value Question. Is X good for Y?
   Is your finding(s) X good for another situation or problem Y?
2. Intrinsic Value Question. Is X good in itself?
   Is your finding(s) X good enough without further research Y?
3. Comparative Value Question. Is X better than Y?
   Is your finding(s) X better than another similar event Y?

4. Decision Value Question. Is X right? Ought we choose X?
   Is your finding(s) X satisfactory? Is there a better alternative Y?
5. Ideal Value Question. Is X as good as it can be, or can it be made much better ideally?

Is your finding(s) X the final answer? Can you think of a better resolution?

Once you have answered the value claim questions that relate to your study, take time to *reflect* on your overall research effort. *Review the following statements and questions and write your responses.*

1. State the significance of your research findings.
2. Does your research have practical implications to the area you studied?
3. Do your research findings help you to have a better grasp of the topic?
4. Will someone else reading your research report learn from your work?
5. What do you consider to be the primary meaning of this investigation?

V

ACTION

The intent of the action phase shown on the following page is to start thinking about a future study that can either help to answer a question or hypothesis that may not have been clear given the way it was asked or stated or perhaps the events may need to be refined and/or the records. Or perhaps this study has suggested a question that you feel you need to know more about that will either satisfy your curiosity or extend what is now known with what can be.

Research Strategy

FORMULATION

Formulate an idea or problem to study

World View: The general belief system motivating and guiding the inquiry.

Philosophy: The beliefs about the nature of knowledge and knowing guiding the the inquiry.

Relationship: Relate the idea or problem to previous studies (literature review), prior knowledge, and experience.

Purpose: Explanation of the purpose of the research Project

Aims of Project: Accomplishments that are foreseen

Value Claims: What do you foresee as the worth of this study?

Theory: The general principles guiding the inquiry about events and/or objects that explains why events or objects exhibit what is observed.

Concepts: Perceived regularity in events or objects designated by a label.

Principles: Statements of relationship between concepts that explain how events or objects can be expected to appear or behave.

Constructs: Ideas showing specific relationships between concepts without direct

Research Question: Questions that serves to focus the inquiry about events and/or objects studied.

DESIGN

Event/Object: Description of the event and /or object) to be studied in order to answer the focus question

- Subjects
- Situation
- Treatment
- Procedure
  - (modify)
  - (revise)

Records: The Observations made and instruments used to record the events and/or objects studied.

ANALYSIS

Transformations: The analysis and organization of the data (e.g., tables, graphs, charts, concept maps, or other forms of organization of records)

FINDINGS

Knowledge Claims: Statements that answer the focus question and are reasonable interpretations of the records and transformed records (or data) obtained

REFLECTIONS

Value Claims: Statements Based on Knowledge claims that declare the worth or value of the inquiry.

Presentation of evidence and links to the next study (i.e. review, reflect, evaluate, and improve practice).

Chapter 9

Acting on the Next Steps

The ideal reasoner would, when he has once been shown a single fact in all its bearing, deduce from it not only all the chain of events which led up to it, but also all the results which would follow from it.

—(The Five Orange Pips)

Presenting evidence linking to the next study (i.e., review, reflect, evaluate, improve practice or extend knowledge) of the event(s) or object(s).

1. *New questions.*
2. *Key concepts that may need redefining.*
3. *Evidence for further research.*
4. *Imagining unrealized possibilities.*

RETHINKING PROCESS

1. What new questions do the data make you think of?
2. Can the key concepts be redefined?
3. Use the evidence that you have gathered and link it to a follow-up investigation.
4. As you reflect on the outcome of your research study, *think* and *imagine* what can be done to advance the knowledge and understanding of your findings.
5. What unrealized possibilities can you imagine?

Chapter 10

Writing Your Research Report, Article, Master's Thesis, Doctoral Dissertation

Education never ends.

—(The Adventure of the Red Circle)

1. *Reviewing your notes from each of the phases in the research strategy.*
2. *Organizing and writing your research report, article, master's thesis, or doctoral dissertation.*
3. *New questions to consider.*

You are now ready to write and share your work with others. How you organize and write your research paper is important for several reasons. First, you have made new knowledge with your investigation. Second, you want to organize what you did and found so that it makes sense to you. Third, you want to write a paper so that it is readable and has meaning for others.

If you used either the concept mapping procedure and/or the **V** diagram during your study, they can be used to organize and write your research paper. For example, you may wish to make a concept map of your research paper as you begin, and then use it as a template from which to write your paper. If you have been developing concept maps during your study, this should be a culminating map that includes your answers to those pertinent questions of plan/strategy, course of action, resolution, and action. Also, the **V** diagram is another way to organize and write your research paper. All of the elements necessary to write a comprehensive paper are contained within the **V** diagram. We are better able to visualize the merits or shortcomings of an experiment or a research report by writing our reactions. The paper is more exact and contains far more pertinent information

49

than simply listing the facts or results. By incorporating the elements arrayed around the **V** diagram it serves as the basis for writing the paper.

1. REVIEWING YOUR NOTES FROM EACH OF THE PHASES IN THE RESEARCH STRATEGY

Gather your notes from plan/strategy, course of action, and resolution. These include answers to the questions you wrote. Begin to visualize a conceptual framework of your paper.

2. ORGANIZING AND WRITING YOUR RESEARCH REPORT, ARTICLE, MASTER'S THESIS, OR DOCTORAL DISSERTATION

a. Use your notes from Plan/Strategy to begin writing:

* Introduction
* Review of the Literature
* Research Questions/Hypotheses

b. Use your notes from Course of Action to write this section:

* Describe what you did to answer your question(s).
* Describe the records you used to collect the "facts."

c. Use your notes from Resolution to write this section:

* What were your findings?
* Explain your interpretations and display of the findings.
* Explain whether or not your findings answered your questions.
* What value claims can be made of your findings?

d. Are your interpretations presented in a coherent and organized manner?
e. Do you think that someone else reading your interpretation of the report or paper can learn something as a result of your work?

3. NEW QUESTIONS TO CONSIDER

What further action should be recommended to extend this research? Be sure to review and include your thoughts with the action phase when writing this section.

Epilogue

As a researcher, it is important to be mindful of the various landscapes that the problem or situation offers. A goal is to view its complexities without denying them and to simplify them so that they can be better known and understood.

We hope that the journey you have taken has shed light on the path and provided an opportunity to conceptualize your ideas. You have forged paths of inquiry that lead to a better understanding of a piece of knowledge. If you used the **V** diagram, you have constructed and deconstructed the structure of knowledge of a given piece of a problem or a situation. Using concept maps have aided in organizing and revealing your ideas. Sharing these ideas with others and negotiating meaning is vital in this research endeavor. Remaking your maps resulted in rethinking your ideas and crystallizing them into a focused path of inquiry.

You have changed your meaning of experience with the journey. This change will now enable you to go forward and change future meanings. The road to unrealized possibilities is beckoning.

Appendices

CHECKING YOUR PROGRESS

It is important that a schedule be followed when planning and carrying out your research investigation. Several venues are provided for this to occur. One is following the phases of the Research Strategy and using the *Researcher Checklist,* Appendix A. Another is having meetings with your teacher/professor or committee members to enable you to check your progress and determine the next phase of study by also using the *Researcher/ Mentor Checklist,* Appendix B. The concept maps and **V** diagrams you are constructing along with the feedback you receive are also enablers in the research process.

The *Researcher Checklist* is designed to keep track and record progress with your investigation. Notice that the *Researcher Checklist* is not sequential. Keep a record of when you begin the study, the pathways you take toward a resolution, and reaching a resolution. Items that appear in *italics* are for those researchers who are working with a teacher, professor, mentor researcher, or committee members.

The *Researcher/Mentor Checklist* is designed to keep track of progress of your investigation if you are a student/researcher under the guidance of your teacher/professor, mentor researcher, or committee members.

Appendix A

Researcher Checklist

Student's Name: _____ Classification: _____ Academic Year: _____

Check	Topic	Date Completed
	Read the Entire Book	
	Reread Research Phases – Think about possible Problem/Situation – Think about a potential Plan/Strategy – Think about ideas for Course of Action – Start Assembling your documents and materials.	
	– Meet with teacher/professor/researcher	
	– Select a topic for your research	
	RESEARCH STRATEGY	
	– Reread Research Strategy	
	– Completed Problem/Situation	
	– Completed Plan/Strategy	
	– Complete Course of Action	
	– Completed Resolution	
	– Completed Action	

	Concept Maps	
	– Initiate Concept Map	
	– Completed Concept Map	
	– *Send for Review and Feedback*	
	– Revised Concept Map	
	Interactive V Diagrams	
	– Initiate **V** Diagram	
	– Completed Phase I	
	– *Send for Review and Feedback*	
	– Revised **V** Diagram	
	– *Send for Review and Feedback*	
	– Completed **V** Diagram	
	– *Send for Review and Feedback*	
	– *Received Feedback*	
	Writing Your Research Report	
	– Review items for inclusion using your final **V** Diagram as a template	
	– First Draft	
	– Second Draft	
	– Final Report	

Appendix B

Researcher/Mentor Checklist

Student's Name: _____ Classification: _____Academic Year: _____

Check	Topic	Date Completed
	Initial Meeting	
	– Met with student	
	– Discussed preliminary research project	
	STUDENT RESEARCH PROJECT	
	– A research topic has been agreed upon.	
	– Expectations have been explained and understood by the student.	
	– Meeting schedule with student has been established.	
	Student Progress	
	– Student is communicating via an electronic journal or visitation.	
	– Student has submitted a Problem/Situation for investigation.	
	– Problem/Situation is approved.	
	– Student has submitted a Plan/Strategy for conducting research investigation.	

	– Plan/Strategy is approved	
	– Student has submitted a Course of Action for the research investigation.	
	– Course of Action is approved.	
	– Completed Course of Action	
	– Completed Resolution	
	– Completed Action	
	Concept Maps	
	– Student has submitted the first concept map.	
	– Concept Map has been Reviewed and Feedback given to student.	
	– Revised concept map has been submitted.	
	– Concept Map Reviewed and Feedback given to student on this revision. (Depending on number of concept maps developed during the research project, each final one is recorded after completion.)	
	– Record of Additional Concept Maps Completed by Student.	
	– Final Concept Maps Approved	
	Interactive V Diagrams	
	– Student has submitted the first stage of the V Diagram.	
	– Phase I of the V Diagram Reviewed with Feedback.	
	– Student Revised V Diagram submitted for review.	
	– Feedback given on revised V Diagram.	
	– Phase II of V Diagram submitted for Review.	
	– V Diagram approved or Feedback given to student for revision.	
	– Final V Diagram approved.	

	Research Report	
	– Review to ascertain that required items are included in research report. If necessary, either send feedback via electronic journal or meet with student.	
	– First Draft has been reviewed and feedback given.	
	– Second Draft has been reviewed and feed-back given	
	– Final Report is approved.	

About the Authors

Marino C. Alvarez is a professor in the Department of Teaching and Learning of the College of Education and a senior researcher and Director of the Exploring Minds Project, in the Center of Excellence in Information Systems at Tennessee State University. His master's and doctoral degrees are from West Virginia University. He has served on international and national committees, editorial advisory boards, and was a Past President of the College Reading Association and Past Chair of the Action Research Special Interest Group of the American Educational Research Association. Dr. Alvarez is a coauthor with Bob Gowin of *The Art of Educating with V Diagrams* published by Cambridge University Press. Professor Alvarez is the only recipient of both the *Teacher-of-the-Year* and the *Distinguished Researcher-of-the-Year* Awards at Tennessee State University.

D. Bob Gowin was a professor at Cornell University, Stanford University, and The University of Chicago. He specializes in philosophy, psychology, and pedagogy. He has been listed in Who's Who, Leaders in Education. He won year-long fellowships from Yale University and the U.S Department of Education. He has authored fifteen books and monographs *(Educating, Learning How to Learn, The Art of Educating with V Diagrams, Appraising Educational Research)*. Dr. Gowin was raised in Texas (BA, University of Texas), graduated from Yale University (PhD), Stanford University, (MA) and now lives in Northern California. He is a golfer who occasionally competes in local tournaments.